The Book Every Call Center Must Have

Volume 1:

# Mastering the Irate Caller

Joshua Martin

# Intention

This book will give you the tools you need to navigate challenging phone calls while minimizing your stress levels and managing your own emotions. De-escalating irate, difficult customers is no easy task, but with the right strategies, you can save time, effort, and your own sanity.

For those of you who lead call centers, you will find these strategies helpful in creating more positive outcomes from challenging situations, which will help you retain both employees and customers. Instead of seeing these difficult customers as a blockade to progress, you will begin to see interactions with irate customers as potential learning opportunities for improvement of services and processes.

# How to Get the Most Out of This Book

1. Develop a deep desire to prioritize your mental health and to master the irate caller.
2. Stop after each chapter, complete the exercises, and do not continue to the next chapter until you've applied the newfound tips and knowledge to your work/life.
3. If any concepts are unclear, reread the chapter before moving on.
4. Write your strategy on the pages.
5. Highlight the important information.
6. Keep track of every irate caller you can turn around.
7. Write down progress, success stories, and feedback in a journal.
8. Check in with yourself weekly to monitor progress.
9. Reread this book every quarter to refresh your memory. It's an intentional short read so you can benefit from it quickly and repeatedly.

# Dedication

I dedicate this book to all call center agents and leaders. Dealing with dozens of people with different personalities daily is a challenging job that can seep into your personal life. You owe it to yourself and to your mental health to follow the exercises outlined in this book. You have my respect. Thank you for all that you do. You are appreciated.

# Contents

Intention

How to Get the Most Out of This Book

Dedication

Preface

1 The Aha Moment

2 The Dark Side of Call Centers

3 You Can Satisfy Most People Most of the Time

4 It's Not What You Say, It's How You Say It

5 Don't Take It Personally

6 Active Listening

7 Empathy and Apology

8 Visualization

9 Knowledge Is Power

10 Solution

11 Appreciation

12 Stress Prevention and Management

13 Closing

# Preface

**"All roads lead to customer loyalty."**

– Joshua Martin

Before we delve into the main reason I felt compelled to write this book, it's important to understand how paramount and indispensable customer service is in business today.

Positive customer service experiences can generate business growth by garnering loyal customers. Customer loyalty is the direct result of a business consistently meeting and exceeding their consumer's expectations. Loyal customers are not easily swayed by lower prices or availability offered by competitors. They would rather pay more and ensure the same quality service and products they know and love. In fact, 80% of customers are willing to pay more for a better customer experience. Now, hold onto your seat. I'll say this loud for the people in the back.

The latest statistics from *Fundera* show that 65% of a company's business…

Comes.

From.

Existing.

(Almost there)

Customers!

(Holy S*%t)

This is a jaw dropping insight that I hope shakes you to the core. You may be asking yourself, "Why doesn't every business know this and why isn't every business striving for customer retention and customer loyalty?" Hmmm ... that's a great question that I often ask myself.

So now that you know how critical customer loyalty is to success, how do you achieve it? Businesses need to start investing in improving their customer service because it is their most valuable marketing asset.

Many companies see customer service as an expense rather than an investment in customer retention. This is a big mistake. Huge!

It's no secret that customers share their positive experiences with others; 11 others to be exact. And of course, negative experiences affect consumer behavior as well. A recent Harris Interactive Survey discovered that 89% of respondents who had recently switched from a business to its competitor did so because of poor customer service. What alarms me about this statistic is that 96% of the respondents that switched did not communicate with the business about their issue before going elsewhere. This means that a typical business will only hear from 4% of their dissatisfied customers while the other 96% pull a Houdini and quietly disappear. If that's not enough to snatch the wig off your head, I don't know what is!

On average, consumers share their negative experiences with 20 people and those 20 people share the anecdote with friends and family. This can quickly result in a proliferation of bad seeds that are planted unfavorably against a business.

In today's social media culture, people can sit in the comfort of their homes and write nasty reviews that can influence potential customers to stay away, or may even scare off existing customers. Social media apps such as Yelp have been instrumental to business growth, but can also work against you. Depending on your rating and reviews, Yelp can drive your consumers straight to you or straight to your competition. Think about it—when you're purchasing a product online, how much do the reviews influence your purchase? How likely are you to purchase a product that has two out of five stars? How likely are you to eat at a restaurant that has poor reviews? How important are ratings to you? I'm pretty sure I'm not the only one reading the comments.

An article from *New Voice Media* reported that US companies lose more than $62 billion annually due to poor service. Holy moly that's a lot of money! This is partially because 51% of customers who have one negative experience will never do business with that company again. You read that right, only ONE negative experience has such a prodigious impact.

A decade ago, I received a coupon from a local dry cleaner, and because I'm a sucker for a good deal, I gave them my business. During one of my garment pickups, I skimmed through the clothes as usual, just to be sure everything was accounted for. To my surprise, my favorite sweater, a black Marc Anthony sweater from Kohls, was missing and in its place was a peach colored cardigan that did not belong to me. I politely notified the owner, and after she wiped the smirk off her face, she proceeded to look for it. As the line of customers grew longer, she gave up and agreed to call me later. After several weeks, visits, and unreturned voice messages later, I finally received a call back. She told me she couldn't find my sweater and that she's sorry but there's nothing she can do. Correction—I added the sorry part, she didn't actually apologize. To add insult to injury, she questioned my intelligence by asking me, "are you sure the peach cardigan is not yours?" I had to take a few deep breaths to stop me from saying something inappropriate. I gave her the opportunity to make things right, I even offered to accept $20, a small portion of what I originally paid, to buy myself a new sweater. That's fair, right? It wasn't all about the money; it was also about the principle. As a result of her poor handling of the situation, I lost trust in her as the business owner and consequently, I lost trust in the business.

**"Just like any relationship, once the trust is gone, it's time to move on"**
– Joshua Martin

The missed opportunity to retain me as a customer would have only cost $20 from petty cash; instead, it led to a loss of a steady stream of business from me. I spend approximately $120 per month on dry cleaning services and when annualized, it totals $1,440. I recognize I sound melodramatic, but this is not hypothetical, this is an actual loss for losing me as a customer. In fact, the actual loss is somewhere in the ballpark of $14,000, as this incident occurred ten years ago and I've been going to the dry cleaners regularly ever since.

Keep in mind this is one small business in a small town, and I'm one small customer. Seriously, I'm only 5'6". Now picture the loss of a loyal customer on a much larger scale. Sixty-two billion dollars in losses suddenly doesn't seem so improbable.

Businesses, large and small, fail because they only invest in opportunities that result in an instant payoff. Getting people through the door is a challenge in itself. Now ask yourself this—if you own a business, what's the point of spending money to lure new customers through the door if you are not going to invest in retaining them? Customer retention and customer loyalty should be one of your main focuses. Otherwise, as fast as they'll come is as fast as they'll go.

**"You cannot run a business solely for profit, you must have a mission."**
– Joshua Martin

What does all of this have to do with mastering the irate caller?

Call centers are multi-faceted and require various agents with a specific set of skills to be able to speak intelligently about products and services, address issues, and answer questions.

One of the biggest problems is that there is a shortage of people willing to work in call centers. How is a business supposed to invest in customer service when there are little to no customer service agents? The #1 reason why call centers have a bad rap is because of the "people aspect" of the job. More specifically, the irate caller aspect. Nobody wants to be yelled at, threatened, or insulted, let alone multiple times per day and for minimal pay. This leads me to the largest problem we are facing in this industry.

Persistent verbal abuse has serious mental health and physical health ramifications that are being experienced by millions of call center employees around the globe.

But there is something you can do to safeguard your mental health without quitting your job. I am living proof that you can absolutely take control of your emotions, master the irate caller, and shift your paradigm.

# 1

## The Aha Moment

I grew up in the city of Norwalk, California. I am one of seven—I have three older brothers, two older sisters, and one younger sister. Yes, that is a lot of kids. I still cannot comprehend how my mother raised all of us single-handedly while working graveyard, driving us to school and being the sole provider of our family. She passed along her strong work ethic to me and I would not be where I am today without her and without the support of my loving family.

I was an independent, self-sufficient kid who enjoyed paying for my own things, even at a very young age. I used to ask my mother to take me to Costco (back when it was called Cost Plus) to buy snacks, cookies, and chocolates in bulk that I would take to school and sell for a profit. After school, I sold chocolates door-to-door in my neighborhood (emphasis on hood) until late at night. There were nights I earned only $2, or worse, nothing at all, but I didn't let that stop me. At 14 years old, I qualified to work for the city's summer jobs program and earned minimum wage, a whopping $4.75/hr. I was a bona fide hustler.

One of my first big purchases was in 1996. I purchased the album "Tragic Kingdom" by No Doubt with my own earnings. The purchase gave me a sense of freedom that I became addicted to.

I had ambitious dreams as a kid. I don't recall how old I was when I realized I wanted to work in the entertainment industry, but when I was old enough to dip my feet in the water, at age 17, I was appalled and traumatized by what I witnessed. I was not prepared nor willing to compromise my Christianity to get me closer to my dream. So much so that I knew I needed a new plan. Plan B came surprisingly easy to me because I was hyper aware of my strengths and flaws. My Plan B was to become a manager of no company in particular and manage a team where I could implement my own strategies, ideas, and one day retire from said company. I was determined, and before my 18$^{th}$ birthday, my journey to realize my new plan began.

After a slew of jobs working in retail and cleaning restrooms at Disneyland, I stumbled into the call center field by accident.

A friend told me her job was hiring and encouraged me to apply. I took a leap of faith and applied for a bilingual customer service representative position at a financial institution, fully knowing I had no previous call center experience nor banking experience. Astoundedly, I was hired on the spot. Little did I know that I was going to become a punching bag for irate customers.

Let me back up a minute. In my personal life, I had always been skilled at conflict resolution, though I didn't think of it as anything that would help me professionally. Sure, I could talk friends and classmates off the ledge, but I never thought it would work in the "real world."

Within the first few days after my customer service training, I realized I was quite good at my new job. The same skills I used to talk friends off the ledge were perfect for calming customers down. I quickly observed that out of 200+ call center employees I worked with, there was only one other agent whom I considered to possess the same de-escalating skills. At the time, I didn't fully understand why I was great at my job. I knew I was kind and was a great listener, but I didn't understand what I was doing different. Nonetheless, I felt accomplished and proud and this drove me to work harder.

After several days, I noticed a pattern after clocking out. I noticed I was mentally and emotionally exhausted. I was drained of energy and kept replaying conversations in my head on my drive home. More specifically, I replayed the conversations with irate customers.

At first, brooding stopped once I parked my car at home, but eventually the irate customers followed me to my bedroom where I kept reliving the conversations over and over. Much like Al Bundy, I would come home and complain about the customers to whoever cared to listen. I talked about them during dinner, during hang out sessions with my friends. I recall bringing them up at nightclubs where I was supposed to be dancing and having fun. I was obsessing over them. These challenging interactions started to consume my life. I quickly became stressed out, depressed, and I started losing sleep. I was unpleasant company and started making poor choices as a result of my declining mental health.

If my reaction seems extreme, let me shed light on how extreme some of my conversations were. I once had a customer suggest that I kill myself because I "sucked" at my job and I was a "worthless piece of sh*t". My livelihood obviously depended on my job so I couldn't tell the customer to kick rocks or go pound sand. I had to tolerate the insults and profanity and I bottled it up inside. The company I worked for at the time did nothing to protect me as an employee. I was told I needed to tolerate it or else. Today, I know how to brush off a comment like that. As an 18-year-old who was trying to find myself, interactions like that took a huge emotional toll on me.

There was an overwhelming sense of disjunction between my professional life and my private life. Between 9 to 5, I was hashtag #winning. I was promoted to a senior representative and then to a supervisor, all within six months of employment. Meanwhile, my private life was bursting at the seams.

After hundreds of personal insults, resulting in several meltdowns in my car during lunches and breaks, I knew I had to make a change if I was to continue to pursue this career. How could I be great at something, yet feel so miserable?

Running away from the problem was not the answer. I knew something "out there" existed that could solve my dilemma. I started visiting the public library and read many books and encyclopedias, all in an effort to cope with and manage my emotions. The problem was, I wasn't sure what I was looking for. At first, I read customer service books, but they didn't help me. They taught one how to provide customer service but didn't teach one how to cope with the emotional aspect of the job. I was already following the basic principles of many customer service books, but something was not clicking for me, so I kept searching. Then, I started reading books that talked about emotions, which lead me to psychology books. This is when my first aha moment occurred. The information I was reading was transformative. I was able to garner enough information to change my approach with customers and even everyday people. Eventually, after dozens of books and experiments with the way I approached conflict, in conjunction with the tools I already possessed in my wheelhouse, I found the perfect strategy with the perfect formula.

Once I applied the formula and witnessed the results in real time, my paradigm shifted. I made a few minor tweaks and adjustments, which I ultimately broke out into two different formulas. One formula for the irate customers and one for everyone else. I was fortified and invigorated. I felt like a different person. Suddenly, I was filled with energy, I had a newfound love for life, and I became surprisingly calmer and more patient. If my patience was cranked up any more, I'd be a corpse. My only problem, which was a good problem, was that I no longer felt challenged—not even by the iratest customer.

After another leap of faith, I landed in the healthcare industry in a leadership role. I started to share my formulas with my employees during our one-on-one development sessions. This is when everything fell into place.

The general feedback the team received before and after my leadership was black and white, night and day. Before my leadership, a customer once told me, "I dread going to [the office] because I know that eventually I'll have to deal with those b*tches in customer service." WOW! Isn't that jaw dropping and scandalous? I was left speechless but truthfully, I understood where the anger came from. I knew I had my work cut out for me. Once I took the reins and implemented my formulas, the overall feedback snowballed into, "Every time I call your office, you guys are so nice to me." Phew! That's much better! The best part is I didn't have to fire anyone. It was the same players with a different game plan.

The two formulas I created can give you the tools to handle any call and any customer. Formula one is to help you navigate through challenging calls, as well as de-escalate irate and difficult customers, while keeping your stress levels down. Formula two provides tools that are helpful for communicating with the average customer (the happy, the sad, and the neutral customer). Formula two is mainly designed to elevate the customer's experience.

Many ingredients in the two formulas overlap, but they are distinct and require different strategies.

This book focuses on formula one to throw a rope to those struggling with challenging calls. A future release will delve into formula two—strategies for dealing with the average customer.

At its core, this book is about mental health and overall wellness. Mental health is incredibly important and plays a critical role in your success. A simple paradigm shift took me from "I am unhappy" to "I love my life." The formulas transformed my life and they can do the same for you.

Are you ready to take this journey with me?

What are you waiting for?

LET'S GO!

# 2

## The Dark Side of Call Centers

Call centers have created a reputation for themselves for having high turnaround rates and for fostering stressful environments that are consequently making employees unhappy and sick.

Think about what comes to mind when you hear the words "call center" and "customer service." You may think of irate customers, stressful environments, and background noise. You may be feeling your stomach tighten and you may think "It's not for me, I couldn't do it." The perception is mainly negative and since perception is reality, I must change the perception in order to move the conversation forward and help erase the stigma of call center jobs.

Unhappy call center employees create unhappy customers. One of the main reasons call center employees are sick and unhappy or eventually become sick and unhappy is because they have to tolerate personal insults, screaming, cursing, and threats on a regular basis from irate callers. This type of verbal abuse is known to cause emotional challenges that lead to stress, depression, and eventually resignation.

The average pay on a national level is $15/hour, which is comparable to driving for Lyft, InstaCart, and flipping burgers at Monty's Good Burger (which are delicious by the way—you should try them if you're anywhere near LA.) In certain countries, customer service agents are paid only $2/hr. Did I mention you can now work at Disneyland (the happiest place on Earth) for $15/hour? I have friends that work for the Mouse and other friends that spend a lot of their free time at his home. If this were a baseball game, I'd say the score is:

Mouse: 5    Call Centers: 2

It also requires a person to wear many hats. We're salespeople, financial counselors, actors, comedians, family, friends, and therapists. You may think it takes a special breed of people to do this line of work, and there is some truth to it, but the reality is that anyone can do it.

Yes, anyone CAN do it.

But first.

Listen up!

<u>You need to master your emotions before you can master the irate caller.</u>
Let the church say amen.

I've been in the call center field for close to 20 years and I've witnessed some of the most tumultuous events. I've witnessed employees get anxiety attacks, sob at their desks or in their cars (aside from me), get up during a call and quit, punch a customer in the face, tell a customer, "Your mother didn't raise you right," tell off the boss, and get arrested for misappropriate use of customer information. I've known people who have been prescribed anti-depressants simply to cope with the stress of the job, some of whom felt as though they had no other skill set to land them a better job. I've seen agents cope with their stress by overeating, drinking excessively (sometimes on the job), and using drugs during lunch breaks. I've seen an agent snorting cocaine at his desk. I've seen peers get picked up by paramedics. And I will never forget the day my cohort physically harmed himself in front of the team—and yes there was blood involved. This all occurred before I became a leader and managed my own team. I have endless customer service horror stories. In fact, I plan to write a book dedicated solely to horror stories.

The studies have shown that when customer service agents speak to a specific number of irate callers, they brood at night about the conversations, which negatively affects their mood the next morning. Agents are suffering from psychological wounds that are seeping into their personal lives, both at lunch and after they have clocked out for the day. Studies have proven that brooding adversely impacts us psychologically. In addition to depression, it can lead to cardiovascular disease.

High demands, unrealistic expectations, and emotional upheaval are driving employees and potential employees away from this line of work. As a result, organizations are constantly hiring and training new call center employees. This causes a vicious cycle—a chronic influx of inexperienced workers decreases the number of seasoned agents, which leads to more customer frustration.

As a leader in this field, it's become increasingly challenging over the years to find qualified candidates, thus, having to hire an influx of inexperienced agents. While it's possible to mold fresh employees, there's a high risk of losing loyal customers and potential loyal customers because of misinformation or broken promises made by an inexperienced agent. Hiring new, inexperienced talent also leads to an increased focus on training, coaching, development, and patience. For other leaders in this field, if you do not have the time nor resources to do so, you are setting the new employees and their department up to fail.

With productivity being a critical piece to staffing and to the success of the call center, hiring unskilled candidates is a major risk because it leaves you with no frame of reference of how many or what types of calls they can handle. You can potentially spend weeks, even months training and developing the agent only to learn that their productivity has hit a peak and is not up to par with the rest of the team nor the productivity expectations. It'll result in disciplinary action, performance improvement plans, and often termination. This is a huge waste of time and resources—ain't nobody got time for that!

Call center work might not be popular, but it can be very lucrative and satisfying. There are many opportunities for career advancement. I don't normally discuss my salary, but to prove to you just how lucrative a career in this field is, I will tell you. I started my career as a front-line worker making minimum wage, and now I'm earning a six-figure salary as a Director. Not only is call center work lucrative, it is reliable, rewarding and can help you develop valuable life skills and experience. You get to solve problems, speak to people with different backgrounds and personalities, and you learn something new everyday. The most rewarding aspect of call center work is that you are truly helping people every day.

Together we can break the stigma of call centers and encourage current and potential candidates to pursue careers in this field, all while taking care of mental health and helping businesses grow.

# 3

## You Can Satisfy Most People Most of the Time

Now that I've painted you a not-so-pretty picture, I think you understand that call center employees take their work home, brood, and become sick and unhappy.

First and foremost, I want you to have an understanding of the science behind the irate caller. This is one of the most important topics I learned in the library many moons ago. Understanding why people get angry on a psychological level will help you approach the situation in a unique way that will benefit all parties.

Let's talk about the human brain for a minute. The part of the brain that is responsible for the response and memory of emotions—especially fear—is called the amygdala. The amygdala is part of the limbic system and is the reason we fear things that are outside of our control. The amygdala evolved to help save our lives, literally. Back in the caveman days, your amygdala is what stood between your life and death. In those days, it was all about "hunt or get hunted."

As Sophia Petrillo from *Golden Girls* says, "Picture it." It's 32,000 years ago and you are busy doing pre-historic things when you come face-to-face with a cave bear. Your amygdala suddenly becomes hyperactive because it sees the cave bear as a threat (duh!), and it triggers the release of adrenaline throughout your body to prepare it to haul ass and run the heck out of there. The amygdala is designed to choose a course of action in situations it deems threatening or dangerous. It will help you fight, flight, or freeze. In other words, your amygdala starts to prepare your body for potential danger even in situations where it doesn't know what the danger is.

In the 21st century, you don't have to worry about bumping into a cave bear because for starters, they're extinct, and besides, the chances of you bumping into any type of bear in today's modern world are slim to none. Unless you're in Palm Springs for Bear Fest (if you know, you know), you may be asking yourself "How does my amygdala affect my life?" It's an interesting question because the dichotomy between prehistoric and modern times doesn't change in relation to what your amygdala perceives as threatening or dangerous. In other words, everyday trivial things such as being stuck in traffic, someone cutting you off, paying bills, or an irate customer can all replace the cave bear.

This is a critical concept to take in. In a call center environment, your amygdala will respond to an irate customer the same way it responded to a cave bear in prehistoric times. It will release adrenaline throughout your body, prepare it for danger, and choose to fight, run away, or freeze. You'll experience your heart racing and stomach clenching, among a slew of other symptoms. Imagine being in this state of mind continually throughout your work day. It's no wonder call center folks get sick. What's fascinating from an academic perspective is that some customers will see YOU as the cave bear and their amygdala will choose a course of action which can lead to name calling and threats. With both people in fight, flight, or freeze, it's no wonder so many challenging calls end poorly.

The great news is that we are equipped with reasoning and decision-making skills thanks to our frontal lobe, which is located in a different part of the brain. The amygdala and frontal lobe work harmoniously together to balance each other out almost instantaneously (emphasis on almost).

I'm sure you've experienced a time when someone cut in front of you in traffic, causing your amygdala to become hyperactive. In these cases, your hyperactive amygdala will see the other driver as the cave bear and choose a course of action—one that can potentially get you into trouble. Thanks to our voice of reason, we have the capacity to tell ourselves, "Don't do anything stupid, just let it go. It's not worth it." As we all know, the voice of reason doesn't always activate in time. Sometimes we jump into action and engage in angry behavior before our mental balance is restored. (We all have that one friend who does this habitually.)

And sometimes the person who engages in angry behavior before listening to the voice of reason happens to be the person you're on the phone with. Before we dig into the tools for how to handle the conversation, let's look at the two main types of irate callers that you will encounter. The first type I refer to as the "strategizer." This is the person who decided, prior to speaking to you, that the only way they'll get their issue resolved is to strategically engage in angry behavior. This is a calculated tactic that people follow because they believe it will be the most effective way to be heard and have their issues resolved. This gives people a temporary feeling of strength, power, authority, and control and possibly a false sense of empowerment. You have to tread lightly with this type of caller because they aren't actually angry, they are fishing. They will throw bait in hopes that you take it, so that they get an emotional response out of you, which consequently gives them more ammunition to further complain and further escalate.

The second type of irate caller, I refer to as the "jumper." This is the person who engages in angry behavior because they jumped into action before their mental balance was restored. Anger can block our logical thought processes, creating a conviction that we are absolutely correct and nobody can tell us otherwise. People may not realize that they are not in control of their decisions as much as the amygdala, which they are prisoners of. This is why actions taken while you are irate are later seen as completely avoidable when calm.

When you're talking to an angry customer, you don't initially know if you're dealing with a strategizer or a jumper. And you may never know. The best approach is always to calm the person down by handling the person first, then the issue. Take a few moments to ruminate on this sentence. <u>Handle the person first, then the issue.</u>

Now that you have a good understanding of anger and irate callers, you can begin to learn the steps that will help you navigate challenging phone calls.

The steps are not in order of importance, and one doesn't weigh more heavily than any others. They are all equally important and all steps must be followed to achieve success.

This is an action book. It's not a kick-your-feet-up-and-chill-by-the-pool sort of book. Read and apply it to your work immediately. When you begin to see results, share the insights with your teammates (as long as you're not breaking any of your employer's policies of course). I recommend you speak to your immediate supervisor if you're not sure. Then see the results filter through the workplace.

You may even get promoted while doing so.

# 4

## It's Not What You Say, It's How You Say It

We've all heard the saying, "It's not what you say, it's how you say it." This implies that how you deliver your words is more important than the words themselves.

Your tone of voice, pace of speech, inflection, volume, and the pauses in between your words are very important because they express more than what is being communicated. In a traditional call center, the callers cannot see you and will make judgments about your attitude and willingness to help based on the way that you speak. Some of the judgment will be conscious while most of it occurs on a subconscious level. This is important to understand because most people operate on auto-pilot.

In the 1970s, Dr. Albert Mehrabian of UCLA conducted studies that suggest that we deduce our feelings, attitudes, and beliefs about what someone says not by the actual words spoken, but by the speaker's body language and tone of voice. He created the "7-38-55 Rule" which states that the elements of personal communication are 7% spoken words, 38% voice & tone, and 55% body language. In a call center environment, all three elements are applicable and present. I have broken each one of them down, based on my perspective.

We'll start with body language, which accounts for 55% of communication. You may think body language does not apply in call centers but that is untrue. Sure, you cannot see hand gestures or posture, but the gestures you use will affect the way you communicate. If you roll your eyes or throw your hands up in the air, you will become increasingly frustrated. If you smile, you will instantly feel more receptive to what the customer is saying, even if they're not making sense. When you smile, the customer can absolutely hear the effects of your smile on the other end: a welcoming atmosphere, a safe space for your customer, and the message that you have the capacity to resolve their issue. You may be thinking, "Wow, that's so simple!" Yes, it is simple, but people easily forget, and some businesses don't remind their employees how far a smile can go.

Think of an establishment that you enjoy doing business with. Ask yourself why. For instance, I personally love going to Donut Friend in Los Angeles because aside from the amazing donuts, I am always greeted with a smile and friendly staff. Sidebar, you must try the Polar Berry Club, it is officially my favorite donut ever. Now, once the donut cravings subside, think of your pet peeves. One of my biggest pet peeves is when I walk into an establishment and nobody greets me. I can understand if it's Christmas season and there are too many customers shopping, but when there are more employees than customers, it's unprofessional. What's worse is when they don't acknowledge that I'm inside the store, and instead converse amongst themselves as if they were on break in the lunchroom. This type of body language does not make me feel welcome. In fact, I feel like a nuisance. I feel as if I walked into their home and interrupted a Netflix binging session. Even if you do not greet me verbally, you can still make me feel welcome by your body language. I cannot say this enough, SMILE. Smiling = friendly = helpful = satisfaction, and with satisfaction comes no need to escalate. In fact, smile in all areas of your life and you'll quickly learn how easily it can improve your day. Smiling will take you far in life.

The next element we'll focus on is your tone, which accounts for 38% of communication. Tone of voice is the attitude behind what you are saying. Your words may not change, but the way you say them does. For example, if you're angry, your words may have an edge to them. If you're happy, your voice may sound enthusiastic. Regardless of how you personally feel, customer service professionals have a duty to put their personal feelings aside and use a tone of voice that is friendly, sincere, and professional.

Under normal circumstances, the tone of voice you use is your natural tone, similar to the tone you use when speaking to friends and family. You are not a robot and shouldn't sound like one (i.e. vocal fry). You are not speaking to a newborn baby and you shouldn't sound like you are (i.e. high pitched). Lastly, unless you are Elvira, Mistress of the Dark working in a call center, do not attempt to speak like a Valley Girl. Like OH MY GOSH, like totally.

Using a tone that is different than your natural tone can come across as disingenuous and the callers may perceive you to be untrustworthy, incompetent, and incapable of helping them. Again, this usually occurs on a subconscious level. This is important to understand because if the caller is convinced that you are untrustworthy, the next sentence out of their mouth will be, "May I speak to your supervisor?"

However, when speaking to an irate caller you must use your inner ASMR voice to naturally calm them down. ASMR stands for autonomous, sensory, meridian, response and if you Google it for the first time, you'll find some of the most relaxing videos (and probably some of the most bizarre) videos you've ever seen. To save you from the latter, I'll provide you with a better name to Google, which is Bob Ross. Bob Ross has the perfect ASMR voice that you can try to emulate when you need to calm an irate customer down. Tone really does matter.

As I said in a previous chapter, I was able to calm irate customers without knowing what I was doing. After the knowledge I absorbed from the psychology books, I discovered that the reason I was able to calm people down was because of the tone of my voice. When a customer escalated their voice, my brain automatically turned off my natural tone and turned on a calming voice without me realizing it. The calming voice carries signals of calm and relaxation which consequently slows the brain down and automatically reduces the customer's anger.

If you mirror your tone of voice with the irate customer's tone of voice, or use a tone that sounds critical, disappointed, frustrated, or snarky, the adverse impacts will be detrimental. Using angry or negative tones of voice can further exasperate the level of frustration, anxiety, and anger the customer may be feeling. Angry tones inform your brain of a potential threat. This is why people automatically stop what they're doing and become hyper aware of their surroundings when they hear an angry voice in a public setting.

Combining the two elements—smiling while using your natural tone or your calming, ASMR voice is the best approach to every phone call, and you must make it your default. This approach will have the greatest impact on how an interaction turns out. You must make it your default. It is the most effective approach. Keep in mind that there are exceptions when you shouldn't be smiling, such as when expressing empathy to a caller, which we'll talk about more in depth later.

Most call centers provide pre-determined scripting for you to read from, which means that the last element of communication, spoken word (7% of communication) comes directly from a script. Scripting is incredibly significant to a call center because it improves call efficiency and the need for extended training. Call efficiency can be achieved by having clear and concise scripting with key words and key information that are easily retained by the customer. It also promotes consistency across the business to ensure that all consumers share a similar and excellent experience.

Written words are absent of emotions, which leaves things open to interpretation by the individual agent. The words should contain a stylistic tone that you can use as your lodestar. The next section is for both leaders and agents. As a leader, you will need to decide which stylistic tone better suits your business.

Let me explain.

There are three stylistic tones to call center scripting.

1) Formal

2) Casual

3) Funny

Different styles produce a different effect. For example, let's communicate a common problem every call center faces in each stylistic tone.

First let's try formal:

"I apologize Mr. Martin, the network is currently down. May I have your call back number? I'll be happy to assist you once the network is operating again."

Your message is clear and professional. You aren't trying to be funny; the message is formal and straightforward.

Now, let's take the same common problem and give it a casual spin:

"I'm sorry Joshua, our systems are currently down right now. Would you like to call back or leave a message?"

The main differences are: I'm referred to by my first name, "I apologize" becomes "I'm sorry" and I added the casual expression "right now" at the end of the sentence.

Lastly, let's make this funny:

"Joshua, I think you broke our phone system … just kidding our systems are down right now. Can you try back in a bit?"

Sure, it's not laugh-out-loud funny but it's definitely cheesy and irreverent.

As a business leader, you have to decide which stylistic tone is better suited to represent your business. A call center for Disney may get away with being funny, but jokes in a formal environment can end up insulting your customer. You don't have to limit your business to just one style—you can choose two or use all three, but you must prioritize them. For example, in a hospital setting where you are dealing with sick patients or family members who have lost a loved one, it's more appropriate to select formal as your primary style and casual as your secondary. You can toggle back and forth between the two style tones as you deem appropriate, keeping in mind that formal is in the primary position (at least in this example), and should therefore be utilized more than 50% of the time.

As a customer service representative, if you are naturally funny and you feel compelled to make the customer laugh, only do so when you are confident that the caller will not be offended. You have to make the judgment call based on how the phone conversation is flowing.

To call center leaders, once you've decided which stylistic tones are appropriate and choose how you'll prioritize them, revisit all of your literature and scripts and make the appropriate adjustments so that they ebb and flow in a standardized fashion in the style that better suits your business.

Your tone of voice and the spoken words must be aligned or the message will be lost in translation. Don't let your tone of voice or body language contradict your spoken words. For instance, if you say, "I'm so sorry" but your tone of voice reads as sarcastic, the customer will receive the message as such, thus, changing the desired outcome.

The three main takeaways in this section are:

1. Speak using your natural tone of voice or your calming, ASMR voice.

2. Smile (literally) when you're speaking to customers.

3. Call center leaders need to decide on the appropriate stylistic tone, or a combination of the three.


Exercise #1:

Ask your supervisor or a friend to listen (without seeing your face) and provide feedback. With the other person in the room, read the following script without smiling:

"Good afternoon, thank you for calling Joshua Martin Entertainment, my name is _____, how may I help you today?"

Now, reread the script using your natural tone of voice, only this time, smile.

Ask your supervisor or friend which version they'd like to hear when calling a company that they personally do business with. Ask them to explain why. Remember, smiling equals friendly and helpful. It's not rocket science.

Exercise #2:

Follow the same steps as Exercise #1, only this time, read the following script while using your inner calming, ASMR voice. In other words, your tone should be soothing, slowed-down, buttery, silky smooth and as close to a whisper without actually whispering.

"I sincerely apologize for the inconvenience."

Ask your friend, supervisor, or yourself how this approach makes you feel.

Exercise #3:

In front of a mirror, repeat the words, "I'm sorry to hear that" in various tones including sarcasm, frustration, joy, etc. The intention is for you to hear the different tones and find the one you would personally believe if a business representative said it to you. Choose the most believable version.

Tip: Invest in a mirror you can place on your desk so that you can see yourself speaking to customers. If the person staring back looks unhappy or stressed, chances are that's what the customer can hear on the other end.

# 5

## Don't Take It Personally

Anger is a naturally occurring human emotion that we all feel and experience. Independently, anger is not an issue, it's how you choose to manage it. We all deal with anger in our own unique ways. When you're talking to an angry person and your organization caused their anger, you become a target. One of the greatest skills you can possess in your wheelhouse for your professional and personal life is the ability to not take things personally.

The customer's cause for being angry is completely valid. Some of your customers will actually believe that your organization is trying to defraud them and they are trying to defend themselves.

Defense is the standard approach to anger. When someone attacks, we innately go into stress and defense mode and want to counterattack. A defensive approach is counterproductive if your intent isn't to attack but to calm the customer down. You are incapable of helping customers when your judgment is clouded by your own personal anger.

If you allow the anger to build within you, your mind will give you dozens of reasons why you are right and why the customer is wrong. You'll feel as though your anger is justified. Try to realize that the customer will feel as justified as you and that this interaction won't go anywhere positive.

Before we go any further, there's a wildly important caveat you need to know, which is ...

The first reaction is the first thing that goes wrong.

Picture it. The call has been transferred to your line, you've greeted the customer with your opening script, and the customer immediately attacks you verbally. If your first reaction is to take the bait and give the customer an emotional response, consider yourself defeated. You have lost the battle and your chances at recovering the call are slim to none. An example of taking the bait is by becoming defensive and/or taking things personally by saying something along the lines of, "Please calm down."

As I said before, you must manage your emotions before you can master the irate caller. Here's how you can reset your mood and calm yourself down so that you still have a shot at turning the call around.

The second you feel anger rising within you, follow the Emergency Reset Method. This can be achieved on an active call, while the customer is speaking, by putting yourself on mute or placing them on hold while you conduct this exercise. If you absolutely have to, you can multitask by completing the breathing exercise while further researching their concerns. If possible, it's better to give yourself 60 seconds to pause and calm your system down.

Emergency Reset Method

1) Don't speak (just like the No Doubt song)
    - Correct your posture.
    - Sit in an upright position.
    - Sit completely still.
    - Quiet your thoughts.
    - Take one deep breath as follows:
        1. Inhale deeply for 5 seconds (through your nose).
        2. Hold for 2.
        3. Release for 7 (through your mouth).
    - Take a second deep breath, only this time inhale through your mouth.
        1. Inhale deeply for 5 seconds
        2. Hold for 2.
        3. Release for 7 (through your mouth).

2) Complete the next two actions concurrently.

    a. Visualize one of your favorite memories, favorite person, favorite pet, place, or thing. The intention is to visualize someone or something that promotes joy and happiness.
    b. Smile...............Try it with me now.........Smile...........Keep smiling...........Keep smiling.........Bigger......Show me your teeth........Hold it........Almost there.......Done.

3) Remind yourself that getting angry affects you more than it affects the customer. Using your inside voice, say the following affirmation at

least twice, "You do not have my permission to steal my peace." Be sure to complete the aforementioned steps concurrently. Visualize while smiling.

Repeat the Emergency Reset Method as needed, alternating your inhales from nose to mouth. Don't put too much focus on hitting the exact number of seconds in your breaths. Just make sure to exhale for longer than you inhale, as this sends a message to your brain that you are not in danger. Find the rhythm that is right for you and make sure you practice in a way that feels natural and organic.

At a minimum, this requires 30 seconds of your average handle time, also known as AHT. In extreme cases, this will require approximately one minute of your time, however, it is not unproductive time. In most instances, you can complete the exercise while on active calls, while actively listening to the customer. In other cases, you can complete the exercise while the customer is on hold, typically because you require additional time to further research their concerns. Again, 30 to 60 seconds to cool down is far from unproductive time.

As you complete the exercises and develop a cadence over time, the need to use the Emergency Reset Method decreases.

Congratulations, you have reset your mood, you did not react, and you can now move forward towards a resolution. But this is only the beginning.

Now that you've calmed yourself down to avoid saying or doing something you'll regret later, the very first action you must take is to validate the customer's anger.

Validate the customer's anger by acknowledging it and saying, "You have every right to be frustrated. I would be upset if this happened to me. My commitment to you is that I will get to the bottom of this and provide you with a resolution." Once the customer feels validated, you'll literally hear a sigh of relief.

Most of us have heard of or have had an MRI but have you heard of an FMRI? FMRI stands for functional magnetic resonance imaging, which uses the same technology as an MRI scan. An MRI produces a scan of organs and tissue, whereas, an FMRI produces an image showing the blood flow. Essentially, the images will display the parts of the brain that are being stimulated. Having said that, there are FMRI studies that demonstrate the fact that acknowledging a negative emotion such as anger or frustration shrinks the negative emotion. You may have subconsciously done this before without realizing its impact. Sometimes when I verbally acknowledge someone's anger by saying, "I understand you are upset," I am immediately met with, "I am not upset." Whether or not the customer admits that they're upset (or angry or frustrated), the verbal acknowledgment triggers self-examination and thus, shrinks the negative emotion.

Another example of verbally acknowledging the customer's negative feelings is by saying, "I can hear the frustration/anger in your voice," and follow it up with a reassuring sentence that makes you accountable for taking ownership of their issue and resolving it. For instance, you can follow up by saying, "I'll be more than happy to further research your matter and come to a mutually agreeable resolution."

Ignore challenging questions and comments. These are the kinds of comments that are meant to bait you, and will suck you in if you let them:

- "Are you new?"
- "Does your company only employ incompetent people?"
- "None of YOU PEOPLE know what you're talking about!"
- "Are you still in training?"
- "Did you graduate high school?"

Respond to these questions with a statement like, "I know you're concerned and I assure you that I will do everything I can to work with you to solve this." Whatever you do, don't take the bait.

Here's a list of common mistakes made by customer service agents that I call the DO NOT list:

- DO NOT tell customers to calm down. This has never worked in the history of time.
- DO NOT antagonize them. DO pacify them.
- DO NOT be condescending. DO be respectful.
- DO NOT repeat the words "ma'am" or "sir" repeatedly as a way to interject. DO refer to them by their name and allow them to finish their thought.
- DO NOT say, "Let me finish" or, "You are not understanding what I'm saying." DO say, "I may not be explaining myself correctly."

How the customer is feeling is more important than the facts. It is your responsibility as the professional to see beyond the anger, frustration, and fear. You don't always have to be right. Avoid a power struggle simply by not arguing. If you are calm, professional, empathetic, and serious about your commitment to solving their problem, the customer is more likely to feel heard and less likely to escalate.

Early on in my career I had an aha moment while driving to work. I was driving down Imperial Highway and was behind trailer trucks for most of my commute. I hit every red light for miles on end. I literally had to stop at every cross street. I could not catch a break that morning. I recall being angry and shouting profanities at the back of big rigs (which I admit is completely idiotic). My mind started to play tricks with me and I began to wonder if there was a man inside of a control room watching me from hidden street cameras, purposely timing the streetlights to turn red on me. I know what you're thinking. This is completely ridiculous. When I came back down to Earth somewhere in the city of Brea, I thought to myself, "Um hello ... don't be a fool ... this has nothing to do with you."

I couldn't help but wonder, if the streetlights turning red have nothing to do with me personally, why do I take the customer's attacks personally when I know they have nothing to do with me either? What's the difference? The answer is there is no difference. This silly, ridiculous analogy changed my perspective and to this very day, I remind myself of this moment. It helps me remove myself from the situation in all aspects of my life so that I do not take things personally even though they are happening to me.

RECAP:

1) Calm yourself before you can calm others.
2) Validate the customer's anger.
3) Ignore challenging questions and/or comments.
4) Avoid doing and saying the items on the DO NOT list.
5) Complete the Emergency Reset Method as needed.


Exercise:

Identify your main triggers. Is it a certain word? Is it when a customer raises their voice? Is it when the customer says, "Can I speak to your manager?" What makes you lose your cool?

Identify what your main triggers are and eliminate them.

Tip: For irate customers who are shouters, lower your voice rather than attempting to shout over them. Lower the volume by 25%, then 50% if needed until they are incapable of hearing you over the sound of their escalated tone. Ultimately, they are calling you for assistance and need your guidance, so they have no other option but to lower their voice in order to hear you. I use this method with every shouter and it works every time.

# 6

### Active Listening

The very first thing an irate caller wants to do is vent. In order to achieve this, the caller needs someone to listen, and in case you haven't figured it out yet, that person is you. Active listening can diffuse an escalated situation, as long as the caller feels acknowledged. Active listening and hearing are two distinct actions that are often confused. Just because you are hearing someone speak doesn't mean you are fully present and processing the information. Active listening is the art of maintaining focus on what the customer is saying, without being distracted by your own thoughts or emotions. When you are on a call with an irate caller, you are like a computer system, processing information in an effort to achieve a desired disposition.

By being present and giving the customer your undivided attention, you show respect for them while acknowledging the validity of their complaint. Doing this gives you the capacity to build and win their trust and helps build rapport and credibility.

It is critical to minimize distractions and not let your mind or eyes wonder (cough … cell phone … cough) because if you miss key information, the customer will assume you're not listening, you don't care, and that you are unwilling to help. Customers highly dislike having to repeat themselves. It is important to write down hot key words as the customer speaks, either on paper or using a word document on your computer.

For example, let's say you work for a phone carrier and the customer says the following:

"Hi, my name is Karen, my account number is 90210 and I'm calling because I am being billed for phone calls I've never made. I've googled the area code and it's a Mexican number. I don't know anyone in Mexico. I need this removed from my bill NOW."

The hot key words you should either type or jot down are the caller's name, account number, and the reason for their call. If you missed any of the key information and request Karen to repeat herself, you run the risk of losing credibility. Additionally, you're sending a silent message to the customer that you are unprepared and/or distracted, which inhibits you from resolving their issue, thus losing the opportunity to turn the call around and retain the customer.

There is great power in silence. When you put the spotlight on the irate caller and do not interject, it allows the customer to get everything off their chest. Customers—like the rest of us—have trouble thinking and communicating clearly when they are fired up. The act of talking and explaining redirects their mind to a rational state and will help to automatically calm them down. This alone will reduce their combative state of mind.

For clarification purposes and to avoid making assumptions, ask probing questions and periodically paraphrase the issues at hand.

Here's an overly simplified issue to serve as an example:

Customer: I am extremely frustrated because you charged me $150 for the installation fee. I am not paying it.

Customer Service Agent (probing question): How much were you quoted for the installation fee?

Customer: $25

Customer Service Agent (paraphrase): So, if I'm hearing you correctly, you were quoted $25 for the installation fee, though you're being billed $150 and you'd like for us to honor the original quote. Is that correct?

Clarifying informs your customer that you understand the issue which gives you the capacity to help them. Sometimes part of the issue is that the customer service agent does not understand the problem, making it impossible to solve it. Clarification helps bridge any disconnects between the customer's explanation and the agent's understanding. Until this is done, your customer will resist your input and will keep repeating themselves (and possibly berating you), under the assumption that you don't get it.

One of the greatest side effects to active listening, other than the obvious, is that irate customers represent a source of learning and an opportunity to improve. Use their anger to make positive changes to your policies. Ask them "What can we do to better serve you today, and in the future?" It's almost too simple. There is nothing groundbreaking about it. I've learned through the years that when a customer is highly adamant that your company made a mistake, chances are, they're right and it's up to you to communicate gaps and opportunities to your leaders in an effort to improve processes, products, and/or services.

Sometimes customers aren't asking for a refund or any other specific action—they just want to be acknowledged or hear that you're sorry.

# 7

## Empathy and Apology

Empathy is the ability to sense, recognize, understand, and share the feelings of another being. In essence, you are intentionally slipping into someone else's shoes in order to imagine what they might be thinking or feeling. Empathy is the precursor to compassion.

Empathy helps us cooperate with others, which—in the world of customer service—builds trust and enables us to establish a rapport with customers. This in itself will make them feel heard and help solidify the connection. It gives us the capacity to understand their perspective and connect with them on a different level, which helps propel you to a satisfactory outcome.

In my career, I've approached empathy in various methods during phone conversations with irate callers. I've completely omitted empathy altogether, I've overutilized it, underutilized it, and eventually found the most effective approach of which I call "on-the-spot empathy."

My on-the-spot empathy approach has consistently defused irate clients, who started out yelling and ended up calmly trusting my guidance and accepting my solutions for resolution.

So what is on-the-spot empathy? While the client is talking and explaining their issues, aside from actively listening, you must actively empathize and apologize.

One of the most powerful and impactful phrases you can say in a phone conversation with an irate customer is, "I'm sorry." Saying sorry doesn't equate to admitting fault and it does not equate to a sign of weakness. It means taking ownership and committing to resolving the issues.

Here are a few phrases you can mix and match while expressing empathy and apologizing:

"I understand," "I'm very sorry to hear that," "I apologize for the inconvenience," "I'm sorry that happened," "I completely understand your frustration," "I would be frustrated as well," "I'm so sorry you're going through this," "I hear what you're saying," and "Thank you for your patience while we sort this out."

Never say, "I'm sorry you feel that way," as it implies it's their issue and you did nothing wrong.

It's important to respond with on-the-spot empathy when you hear a pause in the customer's tirade, rather than staying silent until the caller finishes venting. The caller can go on a two-minute rant if you allow them to, and if your only response is, "I'm sorry," it becomes less effective and may come off as insincere (which causes you to lose the caller's trust).

When you apologize, it's highly likely that your apology will not be completely genuine—don't feel bad about this. You do not know the caller personally and you are not emotionally invested in their wellbeing. In spite of this, try to keep in mind that the more genuine your apology sounds, the more effective this exercise becomes. I recognize that what I'm suggesting is a form of performance art. If acting is not part of your repertoire, the next chapter will give you tools for how to relate to the irate customer in a way that is both empathetic and genuine.

Offering an apology to an irate customer isn't easy or natural for many of us. Remember—practice makes perfect. Complete the following exercises until you have mastered them, and you'll be amazed at the result:

Exercise #1: Crank up your acting skills and record yourself saying the following phrase. Note: it may help to pretend you are saying it to a close friend or a loved one.

> "I am very sorry to hear about your experience. I'll be more than happy to look into this for you and provide a resolution."
>
> Play it back. If you can sell the fact that you are truly sorry and happy to help, then you've got a winner. Much like actors doing voice over, they have to repeat the same line multiple times in different tones and

emotions to give the director different options. Continue to record yourself until you have a believable version. Once you decide, apply it to every phone call as applicable.

Exercise #2: Ask your supervisor or a friend to role play as the irate caller and read the following paragraph to you while you exercise on-the-spot empathy. Each time they express being inconvenienced in any way, respond with on-the-spot empathy. Chime in when you hear a natural pause (represented in the following paragraph by asterisks). Do not wait until the very end of the rant to express empathy.

"I am extremely frustrated with your company. I never received a bill from you and now you charged me a late fee. * I cannot afford to pay more. I'm going through a lot right now financially and the late fees are not helping. * It's been a really rough year for me. A family member just died and I've been left with a lot of expenses. * My kids have been sick and now I have steep doctor bills. I don't know what to do. * Your company clearly doesn't care. You clearly don't care. This is not my fault. You need to reverse the fees immediately. This is ridiculous. I am so frustrated right now."

Give yourself a round of applause if you responded with on-the-spot empathy three to five times. If not, try it again until you get within the range.

Exercise #3: Think of a common issue you're faced with at work and ask yourself the following questions:

1) How would I feel in this situation?
2) What would I expect from a call center agent?
3) What information would help me?

Empathy may not change the irate customer's behavior but it's your best shot. Plus, empathy helps create peace within ourselves during a situation we cannot control.

"Empathy is the most precious human quality." – The Dalai Lama

# 8

## Visualization

We are not all born actors, but that shouldn't get in the way of our ability to empathize. In fact, genuine empathy is likely to be more effective because it comes from the heart. This chapter will teach visualization, which will help you relate to the caller by conjuring up genuine empathy for them.

Visualization will help you invite empathy to flow throughout your body, immediately putting yourself in the customer's shoes.

Think about how you naturally react to a friend or loved one who is venting to you about personal issues. To be more specific, picture your favorite human on Earth venting to you about deep personal heartaches. Think about how you naturally listen empathetically and offer advice and/or a shoulder to cry on. Now, imagine that the irate caller is your favorite human. You'll quickly begin to see the issue from a different perspective. You'll start to see the issues as if they were your own.

We tend to put the blame on the customer's attitude rather than the issue that's driving it. By visualizing a loved one, you become a part of the same team and can find a desire to tackle the issues together. Your brain doesn't know that your visualization is fabricated—it will not know reality from your mind's cinema. As you visualize one of your favorite human beings on this earth, you will feel a rush of empathy towards the irate caller.

I personally visualize my mother during difficult calls. This helps me build up compassion within. For instance, let's say the irate caller is angry because they were asked to submit scanned documents online via the company website or phone app and the company has no record of the paperwork. My mother is not technologically savvy and I can understand if she made an honest mistake while uploading documents.

I then ask myself, "Am I treating this caller the way I would want a customer service agent to treat my mother?" This technique was a game changer for me.

If you find yourself becoming impatient, ask yourself, "How would I react if I overheard someone being impatient with my mother?" The chances are, you will correct your attitude. It's simplistic but very effective. This strategy will enable you to dismiss the customer as the problem and shift the blame to the customer's issue so that you and the customer can be part of the same team and work towards resolving the issues together.

Write the following sentence down until it is embossed in your memory:

**When you feel empathy for someone, it is impossible to be angry at them.**

Tip: Have a picture of your favorite human and place it on your desk. Visualization helps when you have a picture right in front of you.

# 9

## Knowledge Is Power

The call center agent's expertise is critical in your journey to a resolution. Nothing agitates customers more than a customer service agent who doesn't know what they're talking about. I cannot say this enough. Know what you are selling.

If you are in the business of selling a product over the phone, a customer may hear your sales pitch if they feel like being nice, but they will not purchase from you if they don't think you know your stuff. Think about the last time you called an 800 number and thought to yourself, "This person doesn't know what the hell they're talking about." You may have hung up and called back, hoping to get another representative on the line. You may have asked to speak to a supervisor. Either way, the person you spoke with did not do enough to convince you that they were capable of helping.

So, learn everything you can about what your company has to offer. Once you have that knowledge, you don't automatically gain the trust your customers. In order for a customer to believe that you're legit, you need to speak with confidence. You can be a seasoned employee, you can even be the trainer for new hires, but if you do not speak with conviction or sound confident, the likelihood of the customer trusting your word will be slim to none. Even if you are inexperienced and still climbing the mountain of knowledge, you must have conviction when providing an explanation and/or selling a product.

Think about a recent product that you purchased that you are absolutely gaga over and think of the excitement in your voice when you share it with friends and family. The last product I purchased that I was over the moon about was an air fryer. When I tell people about how much I love it, the excitement in my voice alone results in sales. I know friends and family that have purchased an air fryer because of my "sales pitch." That level of excitement exists because I believe in the product. The same level of enthusiasm needs to exist when you are selling your organization's products literally and figuratively. Enthusiasm will only exist if you truly believe in it or if you are a great salesperson. If the latter applies to you, you should probably consider acting.

Remember that customers—and people in general—have too much on their plates and often need others to make decisions for them. People are desperate to relinquish control to someone they trust, especially in business, so that decisions can be made on their behalf.

When you speak from a place of knowledge and believe in what you say, you become the trustworthy person they can turn to for information and advice. In turn, you can more easily recommend certain products to your customers, as well as provide customized solutions based on their needs.

Tip #1: Take your organization's policies and scripts home (with your supervisor's permission) and spend your personal time studying them. You may have to invest personal time but it will benefit you tremendously throughout your tenure with the organization.

Tip #2: Avoid using weak language including but not limited to, "um," "maybe," "pretty much," "yeah," and "probably." Weak language promotes skepticism.

# 10

### Solution

When you take a call, you have a zero chance at solving a customer's issue if you do not know what the problem is. Once you have adequately understood the problem, you have to acknowledge it before offering a resolution. If you do not have a working understanding of the issue, continue to ask probing questions such as, "Can you elaborate so I can better understand?" The most effective way to come to a mutually agreeable solution is by asking the customer how they'd like you to resolve the issue.

"How can I resolve this for you and come to a mutually agreed upon resolution?"

Oftentimes, there is nothing you can do from a monetary perspective that will resolve the issue. Sometimes the customer is upset because they need a better understanding of a service, product, or policy. Sometimes all you can do is offer a listening ear, an apology, and educate them in order to circumvent future misunderstandings. Other times it's more complex.

As a call center agent, you must possess the skills to quickly identify if this is a real issue—a gap in a process or a policy that needs to be changed by your leaders—or simply an unpopular policy that you have zero control over.

If a serious error occurred and your organization is committed to being accountable, then the leaders of your organization need to re-strategize and make some changes to their policies. A reputable and respectable business will do the right thing.

Here are best practices for call center leaders:

1) Develop a customer recovery policy. You'll need to determine what this means in your field. Does this mean providing a discount, reversing a charge, crediting a bill, or comping a hotel stay? Write a clear policy that empowers your staff to do the right thing when an error has occurred. For instance, say a customer mailed you a payment and rather than processing it, it sat at someone's desk for weeks, which resulted in the customer being charged a late fee. Your customer recovery policy should outline this scenario and provide instructions on what to do so that every customer service agent is

following the same directive. In this example, you should empower employees to reverse the late fee. Sometimes there is no tangible proof that a customer is telling the truth, and a case-by-case review by management is appropriate.

2) Separate policies by negotiable and non-negotiable. Most policies are negotiable.

- For on-site workers: Color code each policy in standing binders. Red represents non-negotiable and yellow represents negotiable policies.
- For remote workers: Store policies electronically in a centralized area such as a shared folder that has a folder for negotiable policies and a separate folder for non-negotiable policies.
- Separating the policies gives your agents the understanding of which rules they can bend and which they cannot. If there are any regulatory policies that are governed by the state or government, put them in the non-negotiable pile.
- Clearly designating where agents can bend gives them the capacity to keep these "secrets" in their back pockets. If an issue escalates, they can easily pull them out and help de-escalate the matter. This should also help with reducing the number of complaints that are escalated to a lead or supervisor.

You'll likely receive unreasonable requests such as, "I demand you to forgive my $10k debt!" or, "I demand free stays at your hotel for life." When clients make unrealistic requests, your job is to focus on the options that are available. If you put all of your focus on what you can offer rather than what you cannot offer, the customer will often choose from one of the available options and feel satisfied.

If you remember my example the beginning of the book, the dry cleaner in my old neighborhood could have benefited tremendously by having a customer recovery policy in place and crediting me $20 (or whatever their policy could have outlined). It could have been a win-win situation. Coulda, woulda, shoulda!

Amazon is known for having excellent customer retention policies. For example, when I do not receive my shipment in time or I have reason to believe that it was lost or stolen, they always make things right by crediting my bill. In turn, I continue to do business with them and spend thousands each year on top of paying for an annual membership fee. Yes, I'm a proud shopaholic! I am also very happy to share my love for their services with friends and family. This is an excellent example of a company that has very clear customer retention policies in place.

Once your leaders implement a clear customer retention policy, start to track and trend the issues. As an employee, you should communicate trends, patterns, and frequently asked questions, as well as common issues to your leaders on a regular basis.

For leaders, if a common complaint is, "I've been on hold forever," you need to ask yourself if you are staffed appropriately. Your customer demand may be too high for your service team. There are statistics that prove that many callers will not wait any longer than two minutes before hanging up. Thirty-seven percent of those callers will not call back. If you are in the collections business, every call is an opportunity to collect. Thirty-seven percent can be a catastrophic loss for your business.

Another complaint might be that your agents are constantly being asked to process a payment. Is there a reason why the customer has to wait on hold to speak to a live agent in order to make a payment? It's possible that your call center lacks automation.

Even with a solid customer retention policy in place, you won't be able to turn every customer around. Some people are in a constant state of rage and anger, while others have been burned by too many terrible experiences with your organization. In these cases, the customer has often made up their mind before picking up the phone, and no combination of words could change their minds. If all else fails, know your organization's policies on escalating the call.

# 11

## Appreciation

Sincere appreciation is the perfect way to end a challenging phone call. Why? Because you are taking a situation that started off as negative and ending it on a positive note. There are studies that prove that positive feedback outweighs negative feedback. Giving recognition inspires greatness. And in the customer service world, that equates to higher customer retention.

Sincere appreciation is the pretty bow on a gift box that seals the deal. The reality is that everyone likes to feel important, therefore, ending the call with a few sweet words will be gravely impactful.

Sincere appreciation signals reverence, and a deep respect and value for the customer's time and feedback. The customer will feel a sense of accomplishment and that they made a positive contribution.

This is wildly important to realize because human beings have a natural instinct for reciprocity.

Tell the customer how much you appreciate them for sharing invaluable feedback by saying something along these lines:

"I'd like to take this time to say thank you for bringing this to our attention. This could have gone unnoticed. We appreciate you taking time out of your busy day to help improve our services. We value every opportunity to improve. Thank you."

Exercise: Focus on the positive. We often notice when others make mistakes, but it typically takes more effort to notice what others are doing right. Make it your priority to notice the positives.

Fun Fact: One of the top reasons why employees leave their jobs is because of lack of appreciation. It is utterly demoralizing when you're not recognized for your skill set and efforts.

# 12

## Stress Prevention and Management

The road to an emotionally balanced life starts by recognizing that our mental health is just as important as our physical health.

I cannot say this enough. Mental health is incredibly important and if you don't take care of it, it will lead to stress and depression.

Traces of stress are always present, especially during your work shift. You need to treat your emotional injuries immediately upon receipt, rather than ignoring them and allowing them to build. Allowing yourself to get too wound up too often can have adverse, long-term ramifications to your health.

The first exercise at the end of this chapter will help you manage your emotions during your work shift, specifically during a challenging phone conversation with an irate caller. While doing this, you can prepare you for the next call with a Zen mind.

The second exercise at the end of this chapter is your homework. Not only will it help you manage your emotions, it will help you leave work at work. You should not be thinking about challenging phone conversations after they're over, much less, after clocking out for the day. Brooding and ruminating results in stress, and stress is literally killing you. When you are continually stressed, your brain releases toxic hormones that damage your mental performance. This state leaves you predisposed to making poor choices.

Other side effects of chronic stress:

- Harms physical health
- Weakens immune system
- Damages heart and chromosomes within your heart's nuclei
- Causes depression
- Raises blood pressure
- Causes heart disease
- Causes rapid weight fluctuations
- Makes you more susceptible to ulcers, stroke, diabetes, and cancer.

In addition, chronic stress can lead to road rage, workplace violence, domestic violence, school shootings, and broken relationships. There are many ways in which stress can manifest itself. Now, please don't misunderstand what I'm saying. I'm not saying you're going to become violent if you don't make changes. We each deal with stress in our own way. What I want to emphasize is that stress is inevitable and it will manifest itself in some way, shape, or form in each of our lives. This is why it's incredibly important to take care of your mental health.

The third exercise is your new morning routine, which will jumpstart your day with a positive outlook.

The exercises outlined in this chapter help release stress and create a more positive work environment, which in turn, offers better sleep, and can improve relationships both at home and in the work place.

Exercise #1: Visualization during your work shift

After dealing with a challenging phone call, complete the following steps. This will help you produce joy on demand which will help you circumvent stress and mentally prepare you for the next phone call.

1) Once the call ends, visualize the nasty comments, insults, and negative emotions inside of a red balloon that you are holding. Now, release the balloon into the air and watch it fly away. Any stress that was caused during the conversation is now drifting away. Any insult that was said is now in the air. As it floats further away, the contents become smaller and smaller until you can no longer see them. Let it go and don't think of it again.
2) Complete the Emergency Reset Method after every challenging phone call. This will enable you to tackle the next call with a clean slate.

Exercise #2: Meditation after your work shift

It's important to understand that a consistent meditation practice results in long-term benefits including positive effects on brain and immune function. Most people think of meditation as closing your eyes, being in touch with your thoughts, and feeling peaceful. While this sounds nice, it often leads to people feeling like failures if they don't achieve peace or stillness during a meditation session. Meditation—when done correctly—helps you connect with yourself, gain perspective on your life, and become more willing to let go of things you didn't have control over in the first place.

Over time, meditation will shorten the amount of time you spend in an angry state of mind, which consequently reduces stress levels and provides you with a slew of health benefits.

If someone cutting you off on the freeway is enough to make you upset for ten minutes, a regular meditation practice can cut that time down to seconds. Give yourself permission to acknowledge the bad that life throws your way, but remember—as quick as it comes is as quick as it can go.

I like to test my emotions from time to time. I will purposely drive behind the slowest driver on the freeway. I'll sometimes stand in the longest line at the grocery store so that I can perfect the art of patience and letting go.

If you are new to meditation, don't let that stop you from benefitting from this practice. The easiest techniques for beginners are mindfulness meditation and concentration meditation.

Both involve finding a quiet, comfortable space, sitting or lying down, and closing your eyes. Eventually, you'll graduate to being able to meditate with your eyes open even in the noisiest environments.

Mindfulness meditation is a mental training technique that involves focusing your mind on your breath, senses, thoughts, and emotions in the present moment. Put all thoughts of the past and the future aside and focus on the present moment.

Focus on your breathing. As you breathe in and out, you'll see random thoughts come and go. Don't ignore them. Don't judge them. Simply acknowledge them and remain calm. If you find yourself excessively thinking negative thoughts, turn your focus on your breathing.

Try it for five minutes then graduate to ten minutes or longer. The intention behind mindfulness meditation is to be in the present moment (not in the past and not in the future). One of my favorite Zen teachers, Thich Nhat Hanh says, "There are two ways to wash the dishes. The first is to wash the dishes in order to have clean dishes and the second is to wash the dishes to wash the dishes." In other words, if while washing the dishes, you're rushing and thinking only of the Netflix program that awaits you, then you are not "washing the dishes to wash the dishes." Essentially, you are living in the future. If you're not in the present moment during the dishes, you won't be present while watching Netflix either. You'll be on your phone or thinking of the next thing you need to do, robbing yourself of the enjoyment of what is happening now.

Concentration meditation is a technique that involves focusing on a singular point. Some people repeat a mantra, some people imagine their favorite vacation spot, and people (like me) listen to a guided meditation video. There isn't a wrong way to do this as long as it involves focusing on a single point.

As your mind wanders, refocus your awareness on your chosen object. Through this process, your ability to concentrate improves.

Exercise #3: Develop a gratitude habit

Start each morning quietly. Wake up five to ten minutes before your usual wake up time and practice gratitude. Focus on the things you currently possess and make a mental note of all of the things you are grateful for. Personally, I start with the fundamentals, such as my senses, my ability to breathe, see, hear, speak, and touch. I then visualize every person who has touched my life, including my significant other, my parents, my siblings, my nieces and nephews, my extended family, my chosen family, and my four-legged children. There is always something for you to be grateful for. After your five-to-ten-minute session is over, commit to having a productive day.

I'm going to mention lifestyle changes that will help you live a balanced life, but I won't spend too much time talking about the them:

- Eat more greens and whole foods.
- Increase physical exercise.
- Stick to a consistent sleep schedule including the weekends. Remember, lack of sleep increases irritability.
- Avoid eating too late (no less than three hours before bedtime).
- Avoid caffeine after you've clocked out.
- Turn off all of the lights and put your phone away at least one hour before bed.

Living an emotionally balanced life and being able to produce joy on demand may sound like a superpower, but it is an ability you can and will develop.

We all want to be healthy, fit, and reduce stress, yet we don't dedicate the time to achieve these goals.

By completing the stress prevention and management exercises daily, you will be much closer to the balance you deserve.

A QUICK WORD TO CALL CENTER LEADERS:

As leaders, we should work together and support employees by empowering them to manage a work/life balance. Give your agents breathing time in between calls. At least 15 seconds, and longer after an especially challenging call. We also need to invest in our employees' wellbeing.

You don't have control over what the agents do after they clock out, but you can certainly introduce a meditation session during a team meeting, or huddles. If you're not comfortable calling it a meditation session, call it a wellness check or make something up. It only takes a few minutes to do a breathing exercise. If your meetings are usually in the morning, introduce a coffee meditation where you clear the brain fog and commit to having a productive day.

Join me by starting a "Mastering the Irate Caller" challenge with your teams. Use this book as your lodestar and complete the exercises together as a team. Share success stories, examples, and how it's improved your life inside and outside of work.

And don't forget to celebrate every irate customer you can turn around!

# 13

## Closing

A career in call centers can be lucrative, but your mental health is more important than your bank account. It's more important than watching videos on the internet or being on social media, although we waste hours doing so every day while not dedicating enough time to mental health. Is a sports highlight clip more important than your stress level? Is your news feed more important than a five-minute meditation session to benefit your mental health? Is a new Netflix show more important than your wellbeing? I don't mean to pick on Netflix, I absolutely love the original content, but my point is that we need to put more effort on our mental health. We need to start re-prioritizing our lives based on value.

Don't put your happiness in the hands of others, especially irate customers. Humans often seek happiness outside of ourselves, which results in temporary joy. Put your focus on prolonged happiness. One of my favorite lyrics comes from a song by one of my favorite bands, the Pet Shop Boys. It says, "It is not easy/but don't give up now/happiness is an option." It sounds cliché and you've probably heard it many times before, but it's absolutely true. Happiness is a choice. You cannot control what other people say or do, but you can control your reaction. If you can commit to completing the exercises in this book, your ability to deal with challenging, irate callers increases exponentially. What used to be hard becomes second nature. You'll have more time to focus on other skills that you can fine tune, and cultivate. Perhaps leaderships skills, or other career-advancement moves. Follow the exercises outlined in this book and make a difference in your life. Just like body building, stress management is a muscle you need to build and strengthen daily. A peaceful mindset comes with daily practice—it will not happen overnight.

You don't have to give anything up. Simply by re-prioritizing your tasks each day, you'll have the time and flexibility to complete the exercises and still watch your favorite Netflix shows and YouTube videos.

Then, you can spread the word and educate those around you.

Next time you see a co-worker struggling with callers and/or unloading their stress on you during lunches or breaks, recommend the exercises in this book. Do them together.

Together, we can overcome the stigma of call center jobs and shake off the negative perception.

When I coach, mentor, and develop staff, I take them through this journey, which can take a few weeks to a few months to perfect, and it always amazes me to see their growth and newfound confidence. I always feel like a proud papa bear.

I'll wrap things up with this ...

Life is short. It's meant to be experienced and enjoyed to the fullest. Don't give others the key to your happiness. Don't let outside forces or things outside of your control dictate your mood. Don't let irate callers influence your life's trajectory. Take charge!

Together, we will take a journey of never-ending growth and learning.

I respect you as a person, as a call center agent, as a call center leader, and as a supporter of this book.

I invite you to keep the conversation going and to keep in touch with me. Send me your success stories. Send me selfies or team pictures holding *Mastering the Irate Caller*. I cannot wait to hear from you.

Visit me at:

Masteringtheiratecaller.com

Write to me at:

masteringtheiratecaller@yahoo.com

Follow my journey on social media:

Instagram: Joshua_Martin21

Twitter: Martin21Joshua

I am humbly grateful for your support and I look forward to hearing about how these techniques have helped you transform your life and work environment.

www.ingramcontent.com/pod-product-compliance
Lightning Source LLC
Chambersburg PA
CBHW071123240526
45465CB00023B/789